Big God = Little Fears
A Twenty-One-Day Devotional

Yvonne M Morgan

M Zion Ridge Press
Books Off the Beaten Path

www.MtZionRidgePress.com

Mt Zion Ridge Press LLC
295 Gum Springs Rd, NW
Georgetown, TN 37366

https://www.mtzionridgepress.com

ISBN 13: 978-1-968693-14-5

Published in the United States of America
Publication Date: January 15, 2026

Copyright: © 2025 Yvonne M. Morgan

Editor-In-Chief: Michelle Levigne
Executive Editor: Tamera Lynn Kraft

Cover art design by Tamera Lynn Kraft
Cover Art Copyright by Mt Zion Ridge Press LLC © 2025

Table of Contents

Big God = Small Fears   1

Day One: Fear Not.   3
Day Two: Fear of Others' Opinions.   5
Day Three: Physical Fear.   7
Day Four: Fear of Losing Everything.   9
Day Five: Fear of Losing Control.   11
Day Six: Fear of the Future.   13
Day Seven: Fear of Disappointing Others.   15
Day Eight: Fear of Sinning.   17
Day Nine: Fear of Hell.   19
Day Ten: Fear of Not Being Good Enough.   21
Day Eleven: Fear of God's Calling.   23
Day Twelve: Fear of Not Being Loved.   25
Day Thirteen: Fear of Being Unseen.   27
Day Fourteen: Fear of Persecution.   29
Day Fifteen: Fear of War.   31
Day Sixteen: Fear of Pain and Death.   33
Day Seventeen: Fear for My Children.   35
Day Eighteen: Fear of Greed.   37
Day Nineteen: Fear of Getting Old.   39
Day Twenty: Fear of Being a Burden.   41
Day Twenty-One: Fear of Being Scammed.   43

Wrapping Up   45

About the Author   47

Big God = Small Fears

Faith is a deliberate confidence in the character of God whose ways you may not understand at the time.

– Oswald Chambers[1]

Being a disciple of Christ does not guarantee a life without challenges. As we read through the Bible, we see story after story sharing about the hardships that godly people faced. These passages encourage the faithful to trust God and keep going. But how often do we let fear and anxiety weigh us down and keep us from trusting in God's master plan for us? The quote above from Oswald Chambers speaks to this situation. Our faith takes deliberate action, even when we don't understand what God is doing. But sometimes, fears hamper us and we lose sight of the Lord's hand in the situation. So how do we battle these feelings of uncertainty and put our full trust in God, no matter the circumstances?

What Things Cause Us to Fear?

Fears and the accompanying anxiety can strike any time and areas of life, and some of these might develop in our minds, such as a fear of not being good enough or of failing. Others might come from within the walls of our homes: illness, relationship difficulties, or making ends meet. Work can be another source of stress: layoffs, deadlines, or work/life balance. And the world can ramp up the tension: wars, natural disasters, pandemics, or rising persecution of the faithful. I think we experience fears when we engage in the "what if" game as we observe what the future has in store for us. And all these events can happen individually or all at once. There is no end to things that can send us scrambling to hide under the covers, but there is only one thing that can calm the out-of-control emotions, and His name is Jesus.

Exploring Other Options For Solutions

If you are like me, I'm tempted to fix the source of the fear first and in my strength. As you will see, that rarely works well. Christ wants us to go to Him first with everything, even the things that keep us up at night. Acquiring the ability to relinquish the illusion of control requires time and dedication because it contradicts what we learned as we matured. Putting faith in God and turning to Him initially is not a sign of fragility, but of fortitude. Once we master this part of our faith life, we will see all the ways God provides.

---

[1] *My Utmost For His Highest*, Dodd, Mead & Co., 1924.

And the process becomes easier in the future as we reflect on the results.

Have no fear, okay? Maybe it might be better to say, "Let's turn those fears over to God," because He is bigger than anything we might face and even if He does not remove the problem, He will give us His strength to get through it. When we comprehend the bigness of God, we see the size of the fears diminish. Through this devotional book, we will explore biblical stories, personal anecdotes, verses, and God's promises to help reduce the magnitude of the fears that disrupt our faith.

Prayer:

Dear Father in Heaven, I pray for each person who reads this book. May they experience Your loving presence as You assist them in dealing with their fears. Guide them and direct them to the message You have for them. Thank You, Lord, for all the ways You provide for our needs. Bless us and strengthen us to face all the future has for us. In Jesus' name. Amen.

Day One: Fear Not

Verse for meditation:

Isaiah 41:10 (NIV): "So do not fear, for I am with you; do not be dismayed, for I am your God. I will strengthen you and help you; I will uphold you with my righteous right hand."

Do Not Fear:

Those three paltry words sound so simple, yet can be so difficult to put into practice, especially fears that pop up in the middle of the night. During my childhood, most of my family lived abroad, so late-night phone calls often signaled a problem with a family member. The shrill ringing pierced the darkness and set off a panic within our household. We all gathered around my mom or dad as we waited for them to relay the news to us. If someone died, then my parents spent the rest of the night making plans and contacting others to spread the news.

My heart still pounds when the phone rings during the wee hours of the morning, as I suspect the worst. My mind fills with thoughts of kids in accidents, or grandkids heading to the hospital for some illness. In those moments, *Do not fear* is not the first thought that comes to mind, but as soon as the details of the situation emerge, I steel my racing heart with prayer. I remember God is with me and He will give me the strength I need to face the challenge ahead. This process came through years of practice and seeing God's hand at work in every situation in my life.

So how did I develop such a practice? As each fresh problem arose, I looked back at how God provided for me in the past. Journaling helped me because it gave me a record of all the ways God stood with me and gave me strength beyond my own abilities. I also turned to the Bible for answers since the Bible is full of God's promises to us for all the circumstances of life. And it also shows us examples of how God stood with others, even when fear threatened to overwhelm them. History reinforces all the ways God provides for His people. Then, I prayed for God to give me his strength to face the problem or to take the trouble away. And I trusted Him to know the best way because He does not always remove the source of our fear. We need to trust His strength to face it.

Bible Promises:

Isaiah 26:3 (NIV) tells us; "You will keep in perfect peace those whose minds are steadfast, because they trust in you." When we put our trust in God, He will grant us peace to face the fears that plague us.

Prayer:
Dear Heavenly Father, I come to You with my fears and I want to trust in You to strengthen me instead of surrendering to these feelings. Please uphold me with Your right hand and help me. You are the Jehovah Tsuri, my rock, and I will run to You with my troubled heart. Teach me Your ways. In Jesus' name, I pray. Amen.

Action Items:
Write about a fear that plagues you and why it's a problem:

_____

_____

_____

_____

How has God helped you in the past overcome fear?

_____

_____

_____

_____

Meditate and memorize today's verse. How can this verse strengthen your faith in times of fear?

_____

_____

_____

_____

When you finish this devotional, come back and record your successes.

_____

_____

_____

_____

Psalm for fear and anxiety:
Psalm 23:1-6 (NIV) "God, you are my shepherd, I lack nothing. You make me lie down in green pastures, you lead me beside still waters, you restore my soul. You lead me in paths of righteousness for your name's sake. Even though I walk through the valley of the shadow of death, I will fear no evil, for you are with me! Your rod and your staff, they comfort me! You prepare a table before me in the presence of my enemies, you anoint my head with oil, my cup overflows. Surely goodness and mercy will follow me all the days of my life and I will dwell in Your house forever. Amen."

Day Two: Fear of Others' Opinions

Verse for meditation:

Psalm 118:6 (NIV); "The Lord is with me; I will not be afraid. What can mere mortals do to me?"

Fear of Opinions:

My grandchildren love to play dress-up anytime of the year, not just at Halloween and they own all kinds of outfits, shoes, tiaras, and masks to help them with make believe. The little ones find tons of joy in pretending to be someone else. Just spend a day at Disney World and spot kids and adults alike dressed as their favorite princess, so I think we all of us like to pretend.

But as adults, some people use masks to hide their true selves from others. They might seek acceptance from others through pretense because they believe no one would love the real them, or maybe they experience feelings of inadequacy about who they are or because of circumstances in their lives. When we live in a manner to ensure others love us, we give them the power to determine our self-worth.

But, when we anchor our self-worth in God's opinion of us, we can banish the fear of others' opinion of us. By observing Jesus' life, we can gain insight into how to live as cherished children of God. Jesus stayed connected to His Father through prayer and by taking God at His word, Jesus found confidence in His father's love and acceptance, and understood He was a cherished child of God the Father. Through prayer and anchoring our self-esteem in God's grace and mercy, we can banish the fear of how other people view us.

Bible Promises:

Ephesians 1:4–5 (NLT); "4 Even before he made the world, God loved us and chose us in Christ to be holy and without fault in his eyes. 5 God decided in advance to adopt us into his own family by bringing us to himself through Jesus Christ. This is what he wanted to do, and it gave him great pleasure."

Prayer:

Dear Father in Heaven, please help me anchor my self-esteem in You alone. Occasionally, I rely on others for acceptance when I have self-doubt, so please help me see my worth through Your eyes only. Thank You for accepting me and loving me. Guide me through Your word daily. In Jesus' name. Amen.

Action Items:

Write about how this fear has impacted you most. Why do you seek other people's approval?

_____
_____
_____
_____

How has God given you peace about who you are in His eyes?

_____
_____
_____
_____

Meditate and memorize today's verse. How can this verse strengthen your faith when you try to hide your true self?

_____
_____
_____
_____

When you finish this devotional, come back and record your successes.

_____
_____
_____
_____

Psalm for seeing yourself through God's eyes:
Psalm 139:1-6 (NLT); "1 O Lord, you have examined my heart and know everything about me. 2 You know when I sit down or stand up. You know my thoughts even when I'm far away. 3 You see me when I travel and when I rest at home. You know everything I do. 4 You know what I am going to say even before I say it, Lord. 5 You go before me and follow me. You place your hand of blessing on my head. 6 Such knowledge is too wonderful for me, too great for me to understand!"

Day Three: Physical Fear

Verse for meditation:
Joshua 1:9 (NLT); "This is my command—be strong and courageous! Do not be afraid or discouraged. For the Lord your God is with you wherever you go."

Fear of the Plane:
Sometimes, the fear comes from some physical situation or event like fear of bees because of a sting as a youngster. Have you experienced a situation that sends you into panic mode when faced with the same situation? How do we combat a physical fear?

This kind of fear showed up during my teen years when we rode on a flight that dropped thousands of feet in a matter of seconds. The flight attendants brought smelling salts around to help those who fainted. My fear of flying, especially during turbulence, became cemented for the next twenty years of my life. But I never stopped flying and instead flew white-knuckled and with my heart racing. So I experienced a lack of control as I sat on the plane and did not have faith in God's ability to keep me safe when the turbulence occurred.

I became exhausted from the sensation of fear, so I experimented with other ways of dealing with it. I prayed for an entire week before my next trip, asking God to change me and help me trust Him more when on a plane, and I determined I would not ask God to take the turbulence away anymore. Instead, I asked Him to change me and gradually I experienced a difference. With perseverance, I released my doubts to God and now I can fly without fear in the pit of my stomach. When you face fear, God is with you, so turn to Him and give Him your fears. I still recite Joshua 1:9 to help me remember when I sense a physical fear creep in.

Bible Promises:
Joshua 1:5 (NIV); "No one will be able to stand against you all the days of your life. As I was with Moses, so I will be with you; I will never leave you nor forsake you."

Prayer:
Dear Lord, I don't want to be afraid anymore and I want to trust Your promises to be with me and never leave me, even during a scary situation. Please help me let go of these fears and trust in You. Please give me strength when fears surround me and allow me to sense Your presence and provide comfort as I present my fears to You in prayer. In Jesus' name. Amen.

Action Items:

Write about a physical fear that plagues you and what problems it causes:

_____
_____
_____
_____

How can you change the way you pray about the fear?

_____
_____
_____
_____

Meditate and memorize today's verse. How can this verse strengthen your faith in times of fear?

_____
_____
_____
_____

When you finish this devotional, come back and record your successes.

_____
_____
_____
_____

Psalm for physical fear and anxiety:
Psalm 34:4 (NLT); "I prayed to the Lord, and he answered me. He freed me from all my fears."

Day Four: Fear of Losing Everything

Verse for meditation:

Proverbs 15:16 (NLT); "Better to have little, with fear for the Lord, than to have great treasure and inner turmoil."

Fear of Losing Everything:

Look around; shattered homes and distraught faces are a stark reminder of the devastation of loss. For some, hurricanes leave behind landscapes of flooded streets and toppled trees as they sweep away everything and leave people with nothing. Or wildfires create desolate scenes of blackened earth and smoldering piles of stuff that once filled our homes. During times of loss, does faith falter, leading some to question God while others seek solace in Him? Is our faithfulness a result of life's luxuries, or would we remain devout if stripped of our worldly comforts? Let's examine Job's reaction to his immense losses. How did he respond to the crushing weight of his suffering?

Job lost his family, his wealth, and his health. Despite his circumstances, he continued to seek God in hope. The book of Job, despite focusing on the challenges, offers a message of great hope to the world. Our world is in search of comfort and hope, but we frequently search in incorrect locations and soon find out that material things cannot provide us with comfort and hope. Our hope can only come from the Lord.

Losing everything makes trusting God feel nearly impossible. Yet faith can grow through practice. Offer honest prayers, where you can speak freely to God. Do a deep study of scripture, allowing its verses to soothe and guide. Seek support from your community, finding strength in shared experiences. And remember God's past faithfulness, recalling times He has provided. It helps to focus on what you still have with thanksgiving. Learn to trust in God's plan even when you can't see it or understand it.

Bible Promises:

Matthew 6:31-33 (NIV); "So do not worry, saying, 'What shall we eat?' or 'What shall we drink?' or 'What shall we wear?' For the pagans run after all these things, and your heavenly Father knows that you need them. But seek first his kingdom and his righteousness, and all these things will be given to you as well."

Prayer:

Lord, I worry about struggling without my stuff and I no longer want to trust in my things for my hope and security. I want to trust You with them, so please help me let go of my belongings for the better things You have in store. In Jesus' name, I pray. Amen.

Action Items:

Take a glance at what's around your house. What items do you think you can't live without?

_____

_____

_____

_____

How does it value (real or emotional) compare with what God can provide?

_____

_____

_____

_____

Meditate and memorize today's verse. How can this verse strengthen your faith in times of fear?

_____

_____

_____

_____

When you finish this devotional, come back and record what you learned.

_____

_____

_____

_____

Psalm for fear of losing everything:

Psalm 20:7 (NIV); "Some trust in chariots and some in horses, but we trust in the name of the Lord our God."

Day Five: Fear of Losing Control

Verse for meditation:
Luke 12:19-21 (NLT); "19 And I'll sit back and say to myself, my friend, you have enough stored away for years to come. Now take it easy! Eat, drink, and be merry! 20 But God said to him, You fool! You will die this very night. Then who will get everything you worked for? 21 Yes, a person is a fool to store up earthly wealth but not have a rich relationship with God."

Fear of Losing Control:
The sheer terror of trying to dictate my son's life and death remains my greatest struggle with control. The doctor's grim prognosis overshadowed William's birth as we learned he would not live long. Panic seized me, and I snapped into control mode to save my precious boy. Hours blurred into a desperate haze of online research into his conditions, phone calls begging for treatment options, and whispered prayers to God for a miracle. I remember the doctor's somber tone as he explained the surgery option, a procedure that would only buy William a short time, leaving us questioning if it was for him or for us. A wave of helplessness washed over me as I realized I had no control over the situation. All came to naught as he slipped away after only nine days.

In our society, we convince ourselves that we can control life, but we cannot. Our control is an illusion that helps us sleep at night. Once the death of my son forced me to take off my rose-colored glasses, I learned the best thing I could do was to surround my family and friends in prayer. And, when things got tough for them, I pointed them back to Jesus. My job as a mom, wife and friend includes helping others to trust in the Master's plan for the events in their lives in all situations.

I think the most challenging prayer for each of us is to ask for God's will to be done and not our will to be done. So often, I want to control the events for everyone in my family, and with the death of my son I learned that I really can't. Instead, I need to trust every situation to God's loving arms. And when the tough times arise for those I love, I need to pray for His will to prevail and for me to accept whatever that looks like for their lives.

Bible Promises:
Proverbs 19:21 (NIV); "Many are the plans in a person's heart, but it is the Lord's purpose that prevails."

Prayer:
Lord Jesus, I worship You as the blessed controller of all things. Remind me You

alone are sovereign every time I'm tempted to take matters into my own hands and that You will lead me as I press into you. Help me remember to do what I can do and no more and trust You with the rest. I trust You, Lord, because You are good, faithful, and in control.

Action Items:

Why does lack of control scare you and do you really have control?

_____

_____

_____

_____

Does trusting God's control give you peace? Why or Why not?

_____

_____

_____

_____

Meditate and memorize today's verse. How can this verse strengthen your faith in times of fear?

_____

_____

_____

_____

When you finish this devotional, come back and record your successes.

_____

_____

_____

_____

Psalm for when experiencing a lack of control:

Psalm 103:19 (NIV); "The Lord has established his throne in heaven, and his kingdom rules over all."

Day Six: Fear of the Future

Verse for meditation:

John 16:33 (NLT); "I have told you all this so that you may have peace in me. Here on earth you will have many trials and sorrows. But take heart, because I have overcome the world."

Fear of the Future:

Do you ever find yourself lost in the "what if" game, imagining different scenarios and outcomes? Do thoughts like, "What if I lose my job? How will I feed my kids, pay the mortgage, and keep the lights on?" fill your mind? Or maybe, "What if dementia steals my ability to care for myself, leaving me frail and dependent?" The uncertainty of the future can paralyze us with fear, leaving us frozen and unable to act. The Bible frequently addresses the "fear of the future," describing it as a gnawing worry and anxiety about uncertainties, while urging readers to trust in God's unwavering sovereignty and steadfast promises instead. Many Bible verses, filled with promises and hope, can comfort us, giving us the knowledge that we can entrust an uncertain future to a faithful God.

John 16:33 helps us to understand that Christians are not exempt from suffering in this world. When terror strikes at us, Isaiah also tells us to turn to God by entering His presence. Because He is our strong tower of safety. We can't waste time worrying about why something is happening in the world. It is time to turn back to God.

Tomorrow is not a guarantee for us here on Earth, but God promises to be with us always, no matter what happens. Romans 8:18 reminds us that the sufferings we experience now are insignificant compared to the glory that God will reveal to us later. If we suffer now, we know our eternity awaits with God in Heaven. The Bible reveals God's words of comfort to us during difficult times and, by looking for God in His holy word, He will equip our hearts for the future, regardless of what happens.

Bible Promises:

Proverbs 18:10 (NLT); "The name of the Lord is a strong fortress; the godly run to him and are safe."

Prayer:

Help me trust You are in control when my emotions tell me otherwise or when I am scared. And at the times when I can't figure out the words, help me to "Be still, and know that you are God." Be my comforter, my healer, and bring me peace. In Jesus' name, Amen.

Action Items:

Write any issues about the future that scare you the most and why:

_____

_____

_____

_____

How can I give this fear to God and trust Him to protect me always?

_____

_____

_____

_____

Meditate and memorize today's verse. How can this verse strengthen your faith in times of fear?

_____

_____

_____

_____

When you finish this devotional, come back and record your successes.

_____

_____

_____

_____

Psalm for fear of an unknown future:

Psalm 18:2 (NLT); "The Lord is my rock, my fortress, and my savior; my God is my rock, in whom I find protection. He is my shield, the power that saves me, and my place of safety."

Day Seven: Fear of Disappointing Others

Verse for meditation:
Proverbs 24:16 (NLT); "The godly may trip seven times, but they will get up again. But one disaster is enough to overthrow the wicked."

Fear of Disappointing Others:
Have you ever been told that people are disappointed in you? I'm sure I've encountered it before. We'll encounter disappointment in life, but fear is unnecessary. God's word provides many examples of people who disappointed both God and others to encourage us. Even if we fall many times, God will be there to help us rise again.

God's love for David didn't diminish despite the affair that disappointed both God and despite the affair with Bathsheba that ended in her husband's death and the death of their newborn son. Despite Peter's denial of Jesus, God redeemed him at the Sea of Galilee. Jesus' disciples let Him down by prioritizing their comfort over the messages He preached. The Bible tells many stories of people who overcame disappointment and achieved great things in service to God.

According to some, God never feels disappointed in people because of His complete understanding and love for them. Or maybe God uses disappointments to inspire repentance and gratitude in people. If you're paralyzed by fear of failing God, take comfort in knowing you're not the only one, and turn it to God in prayer. Trust God with it and let go of your fear. He knows you're not perfect, but He'll always be there to support you.

Bible Promises:
Psalm 55:22 (NLT); "Give your burdens to the Lord, and he will take care of you. He will not permit the godly to slip and fall."

Prayer:
Faced with disappointment, I seek Your peace, Lord. A peace that transcends reason, calming the storm raging within me. I long to trade my anxious thoughts for the serenity that comes from You. Amidst the choppy waters of disappointment, let Your peace be my anchor. Amen.

Action Items:
How is God's opinion of you more important than what others think?

_____

_____

_____

_____

What can you do to gain more self-esteem from God's promises?

_____

_____

_____

_____

Meditate and memorize today's verse. How can this verse strengthen your faith in times of fear?

_____

_____

_____

_____

When you finish this devotional, come back and record your successes.

_____

_____

_____

_____

Psalm for fear of disappointing God.

Psalm 62:8 (NIV); "Trust in him at all times, you people; pour out your hearts to him, for God is our refuge."

Day Eight: Fear of Sinning

Verse for meditation:
Romans 3:23 (NIV); "for all have sinned and fall short of the glory of God."

Fear of Sinning:
Are you concerned that your sins will prevent you from entering heaven? Do you question God's love for you when you reflect on your sinful past? Don't worry, because nothing can separate us from God's love. The Bible shows how God used sinful people and gives Him glory when they achieve great things.

David was a man after God's own heart before he became king of Israel. But the Bible also describes David as a sinner, most notably for his adultery with Bathsheba.

2 Timothy 1 describes Paul as an emissary of Jesus the Anointed. Before that, he was Saul, a Pharisee who persecuted and killed the followers of Christ.

Rahab was a prostitute and citizen of a nation at war with the Israelites. But God used her to help the Israelites.

And other people in the Bible who sinned but still served God's purposes include:
- Noah, who got drunk.
- Abraham, who lied about his wife.
- Jacob, who was a deceiver.
- Moses, who murdered an Egyptian.
- Samson, who struggled with lust and anger.
- Peter, who denied Christ.

Romans 3:23 tells us that everyone has sinned. God knows this and still loves us, with a purpose for us. When we confess our sins, God forgives us as promised in the Bible. Psalm 103:12 explains that God removed our sins as far as the east is from the west. Once confessed, God no longer remembers them. So there's no need to fear, just keep serving the Lord.

Bible Promises:
1 John 1:9 (NIV); "If we confess our sins, he is faithful and just and will forgive us our sins and purify us from all unrighteousness."

Prayer:
Heavenly Father, I come to You burdened by my sins. I confess and admit my mistakes. I have strayed from Your path. In my weakness, I ask for Your forgiveness and mercy. Cleanse me with Your blood and renew my heart with Your grace. Help

me resist temptation and live in Your light. I surrender to You, Lord, and seek Your guidance to live righteously. In Jesus' name, Amen.

Action Items:

Write about a sin that plagues you and why you fear it will keep you out of heaven:

_____
_____
_____
_____

How has the Bible stories of others helped you surrender the fear?

_____
_____
_____
_____

Meditate and memorize today's verse. How can this verse strengthen your faith in times of fear?

_____
_____
_____
_____

When you finish this devotional, come back and record your successes.

_____
_____
_____
_____

Psalm for fear and anxiety:

Psalm 32:5 (NIV); "Then I acknowledged my sin to you and did not cover up my iniquity. I said, 'I will confess my transgressions to the Lord.' and you forgave the guilt of my sin."

Day Nine: Fear of Hell

Verse for meditation:

Matthew 25:46 (NIV); "Then they will go away to eternal punishment, but the righteous to eternal life."

Fear of Hell:

The thought of an eternal life, even within our Christian beliefs, can be a difficult one for some to grasp. One of our friends frequently questions his fate after death, contemplating whether he will enter heaven. Despite accepting Christ as his Savior, he still grapples with the fear of whether it will spare him from eternal damnation. Are you grappling with the same fear?

The threat of hell serves as a driving force for some people who accept Christ, seeing it as a safeguard against eternal suffering. As a young adult, my mom encountered a street preacher who claimed the world would end on a specific date, warning her that if she didn't accept Christ, she would face eternal damnation. Driven by fear, she sought refuge in the church, where she found solace and accepted Christ as her Savior. Her faith, nurtured over years, became a powerful shield against her fear.

What steps can we take to guarantee our final destination? Faith in Jesus Christ is the key to salvation, as the Bible explains that accepting His sacrifice through belief leads to eternal life in heaven.

The cross, a crucial moment in biblical history, provides a clear example of God's unwavering commitment to His people. Two thieves, their bodies racked with pain, hung on the crosses beside Christ. One scoffed at Christ, while the other, despite a life filled with sins and crimes, begged for forgiveness. Jesus' words echoed in the air as He spoke these words, "Today, you will be with me in paradise."

To accept Jesus as your Savior, you believe that His sacrifice on the cross suffices to forgive your sins and offer you redemption. In John 3:16, we find the promise of eternal life with Christ, a promise that God never fails to uphold. If we have faith in Christ, we can be confident that we will be saved from the torment of hell.

Bible Promises:

John 3:16 (NKJV); "For God so loved the world that He gave His only begotten Son, that whoever believes in Him should not perish but have everlasting life."

Prayer:

Dear Heavenly Father, I am here today burdened by the fear of hell. I know Your love is limitless, but my sins weigh heavily on my heart. Please, Lord, cleanse me with Your grace and mercy. Help me live a life that pleases You and give me the power to resist temptation. I trust in Your promise of forgiveness and redemption. I hold on to the hope of eternal life with You. Free me from the fear of hell and fill me with Your peace. Amen.

Action Items:

Write about what parts of hell scare you the most:

_____

_____

_____

_____

How can believing in the promises of God help you overcome this fear?

_____

_____

_____

_____

Meditate and memorize today's verse. How can this verse strengthen your faith in times of fear?

_____

_____

_____

_____

When you finish this devotional, come back and record your successes.

_____

_____

_____

_____

Psalm for fear and anxiety:

Psalm 94:19 (NIV); "When anxiety was great within me, your consolation brought me joy."

Day Ten: Fear of Not Being Good Enough

Verse for meditation:

Romans 8:1 (NIV); "Therefore, there is now no condemnation for those who are in Christ Jesus."

Fear of Not Being Good Enough:

Yesterday, we confronted the fear of hell. Today, we delve into the unsettling fear that we are not good enough for God, a fear that whispers doubt and insecurity into our hearts. It is a common challenge to feel unworthy of Christ's love, but it is crucial to understand that your worth is rooted in God's boundless love for you, not in your own achievements.

A variety of factors could influence this feeling. One might be from the temptation to compare your devotion to that of others who seem more dedicated, which can lead to a sense of falling short. Or maybe the relentless pursuit of a perfect life can leave you feeling perpetually inadequate, like you're constantly chasing a moving target. Or the weight of past mistakes can be heavy on your mind, even if you've sought forgiveness for your actions.

The good news is that God's grace, not your actions, determines your worthiness. Your trust in Jesus Christ determines your acceptability to God. The truth is no matter how hard we try, none of us can ever truly make up for all the wrongdoings we've done in our lives. Being flawless to that extent is beyond our human capability.

When those feelings of unworthiness creep into our minds, there are a few things we can do to combat them:

- Reflect on God's grace: Recall that God's love is not dependent on how well you perform, but on His boundless grace and mercy.
- Open your heart to God, sharing your feelings of inadequacy and seeking His strength to help you overcome these challenges.
- Open your Bible and read the verses in this devotional that focus on God's unwavering love and boundless forgiveness, allowing the words to sink deeply into your heart.
- Reach out to a trusted pastor, counselor, or fellow believer who can offer support and encouragement. Their wisdom and compassion can provide solace and help you navigate difficult emotions.

Bible Promises:

2 Corinthians 12:9 (NIV); "But he said to me, 'My grace is sufficient for you, for my power is made perfect in weakness.' Therefore I will boast all the more gladly about

my weaknesses, so that Christ's power may rest on me."

Prayer:
Dear God, I feel inadequate and not good enough right now. I come to You for love and reassurance. Please remind me You made me in Your image, and I am worthy in Your eyes. My value doesn't depend on others' opinions, but on Your unconditional love. Help me see my strengths and accept my weaknesses. I know You are working in me despite my imperfections. Fill me with Your grace and strength to conquer self-doubt and move forward confidently as the person You created me to be. Amen.

Action Items:
What reason causes you the most fear when you feel unworthy?

_____
_____
_____
_____

How has God helped you battle these feelings in the past?

_____
_____
_____
_____

Meditate and memorize today's verse. How can this verse strengthen your faith in these times of fear?

_____
_____
_____
_____

When you finish this devotional, come back and record your successes.

_____
_____
_____
_____

Psalm for fear and anxiety:
Psalm 139:13-14 (NIV); "13 For you created my inmost being; you knit me together in my mother's womb. 14 I praise you because I am fearfully and wonderfully made; your works are wonderful, I know that full well."

Day Eleven: Fear of God's Calling

Verse for meditation:
Psalm 73:26 (NIV); "My flesh and my heart may fail, but God is the strength of my heart and my portion forever."

Fear of God's Calling:
My friend once confided in me she feared what she thought God was asking of her. She feared He'd make her stand on a street corner, clad in a bright pink polka dot bikini, screaming about the Lord's grace to passersby. The absurdity of the thought made us erupt in laughter, but there was a chilling truth to it, revealing the core of our anxieties. What if God asks me to do something I'm not passionate about or that I'd rather avoid? Fortunately, we are not the only ones who share this way of thinking.

A quick search through the Bible, and we find the story of Jonah, the prophet who ran away from God. God's message to Jonah was clear: he was to journey to Nineveh, a city filled with those who opposed his people, and preach the Gospel, offering them a chance for redemption. Jonah couldn't bear the thought of assisting them, so he went to great lengths to avoid God's instructions. Jonah's attempt to avoid God's calling led him to a dark, cramped space within a monstrous fish, where he spent three agonizing days.

The fear often stems from the possibility of failure or the discomfort of helping someone we dislike. The point is, if God calls you to do something, He will ignite a passion within you, pulling you toward His plan. We can trust that God will give us the abilities required to accomplish His goals.

There are countless ways to rationalize our reluctance to follow God's calling, but the genuine test lies in our faith and willingness to obey. The consequences of not answering His call to go terrify me more than the unknown itself. There is an urgency in these moments to share the Gospel that is palpable with eternal lives on the line. The promise of a glorious, eternal home in heaven awaits us, our reward for living a life of faith and obedience.

Bible Promises:
Proverbs 3:5-6 (NKJV); "5 Trust in the Lord with all your heart, And lean not on your own understanding; 6 In all your ways acknowledge Him, And He shall direct your paths."

Prayer:
I need the courage to stand strong, the determination to push forward, and the belief that everything will be all right. Please guide me to understand that my purpose is

to allow You to work within and through me, and empower me to utter these words, "Use me." In Jesus' name, I offer this prayer. Amen.

Action Items:

Write about something that God calls you to do and why you fear it:

_____
_____
_____
_____

How has following God in the past given you strength to continue?

_____
_____
_____
_____

Meditate and memorize today's verse. How can this verse strengthen your faith in times of fear?

_____
_____
_____
_____

When you finish this devotional, come back and record your successes.

_____
_____
_____
_____

Psalm for fear and anxiety:

Psalm 145:18 (NIV); "The Lord is close to all who call on him, yes, to all who call on him in truth."

Day Twelve: Fear of Not Being Loved

Verse for meditation:
Jeremiah 31:3 (ESV); "the Lord appeared to him from far away. I have loved you with an everlasting love; therefore I have continued my faithfulness to you."

Fear of Not Being Loved:
Do you sometimes feel you are not deserving of love? I know I can be unlovable, such as when anger consumes me, distorting my behavior and causing me to act out. There is a remedy for this fear, and we find it in the name of Jesus. The verse in Jeremiah emphasizes that God's love for us is eternal and unchanging. Now, let's explore how this newfound understanding can help us conquer our fears, replacing apprehension with confidence and resilience.

When the weight of feeling unlovable crushes you, remember God's love. It's a boundless ocean of unconditional acceptance, a comforting balm that whispers your worth, which is not tied to others' fickle opinions but to your very being, a creation cherished and deeply loved by God, flaws and all. God's love, a gift freely given, transcends your actions and achievements. He loves you unconditionally, embracing you with your flaws and strengths alike.

We can overcome this fear by focusing on God's unwavering love and acceptance, rather than our own self-doubt and insecurities. In His eyes, you are someone of such immeasurable worth that He would sacrifice Himself on the cross for your salvation. "Greater love has no one than this," Jesus said, "to sacrifice one's life willingly for the sake of their friends — a selfless act of ultimate devotion." (Based on John 15:13). Though you may not sense it right now, the truth remains: God loves you.

Bible Promises:
Ephesians 3:19 (NLV); "I pray that you will know the love of Christ. His love goes beyond anything we can understand. I pray that you will be filled with God Himself."

Prayer:
Beloved Father in Heaven. A cold, hollow voice in my mind whispers that I am unlovable, leaving me shivering with despair. During those times, help me concentrate fully on You, shutting out all else. Let Your love wash over me like a warm wave, soothing my soul and filling my spirit with peace. Thank You for the ultimate gift of your love, so powerfully displayed on the cross. May I feel that love daily. In Jesus' Holy Name. Amen.

Action Items:
Write about a time when you felt unlovable:

_____
_____
_____
_____

How can you shift your focus to God's love to overcome this fear?

_____
_____
_____
_____

Meditate and memorize today's verse. How can this verse strengthen your faith in times of fear?

_____
_____
_____
_____

When you finish this devotional, come back and record your successes.

_____
_____
_____
_____

Psalm for fear and anxiety:
Psalm 136:23 (ESV); "It is he who remembered us in our low estate, for his steadfast love endures forever."

Day Thirteen: Fear of Being Unseen

Verse for meditation:
Matthew 18:12 (NIV); "What do you think? If a man owns a hundred sheep, and one of them wanders away, will he not leave the ninety-nine on the hills and go to look for the one that wandered off?"

Fear of Being Unseen:
A wallflower, by definition, is a shy person who attends social gatherings and parties, often observing from the sidelines. To avoid attention, they keep to themselves, a silent presence on the edge of the throng. I see myself reflected in that description. This behavior makes me feel invisible to others, a pang of loneliness accompanying the knowledge I'll miss out on future fun. I believe I'm not alone in these feelings; they even coined an abbreviation for it—FOMO (fear of missing out), a term that perfectly captures the anxiety and uncertainty.

God used the biblical story of Hagar, with its themes of resilience and divine intervention, to help us overcome this fear. Hagar, a woman of no consequence, moved through her world unseen. The relentless mistreatment by Sarah, a constant barrage of insults and backbreaking labor, forced Hagar to escape into the harsh, unforgiving wilderness. Despair threatened to consume Hagar, but then a radiant light and the sound of rustling wings announced the angel's arrival. The visit ended, and a wave of comfort washed over her; she knew the God of the universe was aware of her and her needs. Overwhelmed with relief, she gave God the name El Roi, "the God who sees me," a name that encapsulates the feeling of being truly known and understood.

God watches over us, His presence always felt as the most significant in our lives. Today, the name of God, El Roi, echoes with the same might and power it held in ages past. God sees us, even in our deepest struggles and most agonizing pain, offering comfort and understanding. Each of us is a precious child of God. So next time you feel unseen, lost in the crowd, look up and smile, because God sees you.

Bible Promises:
Luke 12:6-7 (NIV); "Are not five sparrows sold for two pennies? Yet not one of them is forgotten by God. And even the very hairs of your head are all numbered. So do not be afraid; you are worth more than many sparrows."

Prayer:
Dear God, in moments of feeling unseen and alone, please remind me of Your unwavering presence, Your watchful eye on every aspect of my life. Even when I

feel invisible, a silent, unseen presence, Your eyes find me, Your ears hear my silent cries, and Your love wraps around me like a warm blanket. Let Your presence wash over me, a soothing balm to my soul, and comfort me with the deep understanding that I am never truly alone. In Jesus' name, Amen.

Action Items:

When are the times you feel most unseen?

_____

_____

_____

_____

Does the story of Hagar comfort you for those times?

_____

_____

_____

_____

Meditate and memorize today's verse. How can this verse strengthen your faith in times of fear?

_____

_____

_____

_____

When you finish this devotional, come back and record your successes.

_____

_____

_____

_____

Psalm for fear and anxiety:

Psalm 27:14 (NIV); "Wait for the Lord; be strong and take heart and wait for the Lord."

Day Fourteen: Fear of Persecution

Verse for meditation:

Matthew 5:10-11 (NIV); "10 Blessed are those who are persecuted because of righteousness, for theirs is the kingdom of heaven. 11 'Blessed are you when people insult you, persecute you and falsely say all kinds of evil against you because of me.'"

Fear of Persecution:

Sitting with the Kenyan pastor, we listened intently as he shared his powerful story of persecution. As a young man, he kneeled at the altar, accepting Christ as his Savior, feeling the weight of his sins lift. Bursting with joy, he ran home to tell his family. Instead of sharing in his joy, his family kicked him out of the home. He slept in fields and begged for food. But his faith guided him through the darkest of times, never wavering. Over the years, he continued to share the Gospel with those who persecuted him. And his steadfast devotion to his faith eventually led many members of his family to convert to Christianity.

The fear of persecution stems from dread of rejection, threats, and physical harm from those who oppose the gospel. In the USA, people largely enjoy religious freedom, though persecution still occurs. It's possible that non-Christians would ridicule us more than they would oppress us. Scripture foretells a worsening of conditions in the years ahead, a progressive decline into tribulation. Through mission trips and speaking engagements, we witnessed firsthand the terrifying reality of persecution, hearing stories of brutality and oppression.

In every challenge and uncertainty, the ultimate security comes from our closeness to the Lord; His protective presence calms our fears and ensures our well-being. The Bible's narratives chronicle individuals who, amidst trials and tribulations, strengthened their faith in God, leaving a legacy of inspiration for countless believers across generations. That is why, when persecution weighs on our hearts, we can find solace in biblical narratives like the trials of Job or the exodus of Moses, gaining strength and comfort.

Do you fear being persecuted? If the answer is yes, there are two components to addressing the fear of persecution. First, let the fear of God overshadow all earthly concerns, and second, find strength and empowerment from the Holy Spirit's guidance.

Bible Promises:

Matthew 5:12 (NIV); "12 Rejoice and be glad, because great is your reward in heaven, for in the same way they persecuted the prophets who were before you."

Prayer:
"And now, O Lord, hear their threats, and give us, your servants, great boldness in preaching your word." (Acts 4:29 NLT). Help me, Father, to remain steadfast and unmovable, like a rock against the relentless waves of persecution. May I never falter or grow weary in my faith, but stand firm, knowing that in you, victory is certain, a bright light guiding my path. Amen.

Action Items:
Write about a time you felt persecuted or witnessed persecution:

_____
_____
_____
_____

How can God strengthen your faith to withstand future persecution?

_____
_____
_____
_____

Meditate and memorize today's verse. How can this verse strengthen your faith in times of fear?

_____
_____
_____
_____

When you finish this devotional, come back and record your successes.

_____
_____
_____
_____

Psalm for fear and anxiety:
Psalm 91:1-2 (NIV); "1 Whoever dwells in the shelter of the Most High will rest in the shadow of the Almighty. 2 I will say of the Lord, 'He is my refuge and my fortress, my God, in whom I trust.'"

Day Fifteen: Fear of War

Verse for meditation:
Deuteronomy 20:1 (NIV); "1 When you go to war against your enemies and see horses and chariots and an army greater than yours, do not be afraid of them, because the Lord your God, who brought you up out of Egypt, will be with you."

Fear of War:
So many unsettling rumors of wars, filled with whispers of impending battles and global unrest, surround us these days. A few minutes of watching the national news, with its constant barrage of depressing stories and alarming headlines, will leave a person feeling the urge to build a bomb shelter. From ancient clashes to modern conflicts, the grim reality of war has been a constant companion throughout human history and will persist until the Second Coming. So how do we control the gut-wrenching fear of a devastating attack that could obliterate everything we cherish?

The most important thing for us to do right now is to pray. I'm not talking about the occasional quick prayer. I mean persistent intercession for the desperate situations we see worldwide, the kind that fills you with a sense of urgency and compassion. With hearts overflowing, we should plead to God for His world, begging for wisdom, restraint, and mercy to guide governments and rulers.

For Christians seeking to calm the fear of war, other key practices include: deepening their faith through scripture study, feeling God's sovereignty and protection, finding solace and strength in their church community, and remembering God's unwavering presence and promise of hope amidst the chaos of war.

Bible Promises:
Exodus 14:14 (NIV); "The Lord will fight for you; you need only to be still."

Prayer:
O God, author and giver of peace, we implore You, in these times of unrest, to wrap Your protective arms around us, to bring calm to our hearts, and to guide us safely through these troubled waters. Please ease the suffocating fear that constricts my chest and clouds my mind. I hand over this fear, trusting Your plan for my life and country; may Your wisdom guide me. Almighty God, You alone are our powerful defender, Your love a comforting presence, and ever-present help in times of trouble. Bring harmony back to the world and let tranquility fill my soul. Amen.

Action Items:

Write about the part of a war that causes you the most fear:

_____
_____
_____
_____

How can sharing this fear with others bring you peace?

_____
_____
_____
_____

Meditate and memorize today's verse. How can this verse strengthen your faith in times of fear?

_____
_____
_____
_____

When you finish this devotional, come back and record your successes.

_____
_____
_____
_____

Psalm for fear and anxiety:
Psalm 27:3 (NIV); "Though an army besiege me, my heart will not fear; though war break out against me, even then I will be confident."

Day Sixteen: Fear of Pain and Death

Verse for meditation:
Psalm 23:4 (NKJV); "Yea, though I walk through the valley of the shadow of death, I will fear no evil; For You are with me; Your rod and Your staff, they comfort me."

Fear of Pain and Death:
To fear the agony of pain or the absolute end of one's existence is a natural and rational response to the inherent risks of life. Facing one's mortality, the finality and unknown of death, is a frightening prospect. It's a completely new experience, and once it's done, there's no turning back. Among the myriad ways to die, some involve excruciating agony and prolonged suffering. The thought of dying can fill one with a chilling dread. However, this is not the same thing as fearing death because we are secure in the knowledge of our eternity with our Lord.

For a Christian, the scriptural promise of resurrection and eternal life overcomes the fear of death with God—a hope that appears in hymns and shines in acts of love—secured through faith in Jesus Christ. Facing your own mortality and the fear it brings? Turn to God for help. God tells us in the Bible that if we ask in His name, it will be given to us. Though death is inevitable, the promise of an everlasting life in Christ brings comfort and hope, transcending the finality of earthly existence.

The Bible, filled with stories of faith and perseverance, shows how God's presence is with us in every circumstance. God's miraculous deliverance of Shadrach, Meshack, and Abednego from the fiery furnace is just one example of His power and protection. Another story recounts God's miraculous intervention, silencing the roaring lions to protect Daniel within the dark, echoing den. Trust Him to remain by your side, a soothing presence through the agony, and to receive you joyfully in death's embrace.

Bible Promises:
Isaiah 25:8 (NIV); "he will swallow up death forever. The Sovereign Lord will wipe away the tears from all faces; he will remove his people's disgrace from all the earth. The Lord has spoken."

Prayer:
Heavenly Father, I come before You today, feeling the crushing weight of my fear of pain and death, a burden that steals my joy and peace. Please, Lord, fill my heart with Your peace, a calm that surpasses all understanding, and reminds me of Your victory over death. Grant me the strength to face the unknown, the path ahead shrouded in mist, but knowing that even in the shadow's valley of death, You stand

beside me. Help me find meaning and joy every day, embracing Your plan with faith and love, and live each moment to the fullest. Amen.

Action Items:

What specifically about death do you fear?

_____
_____
_____
_____

Who can you talk with and share your fears?

_____
_____
_____
_____

Meditate and memorize today's verse. How can this verse strengthen your faith in times of fear?

_____
_____
_____
_____

When you finish this devotional, come back and record your successes.

_____
_____
_____
_____

Psalm for fear and anxiety:

Psalm 94:18 (NIV); "When I said, 'My foot is slipping,' your unfailing love, Lord, supported me."

Day Seventeen: Fear For My Children

Verse for meditation:

Zephaniah 3:17 (NLT); "For the Lord your God is living among you. He is a mighty savior. He will take delight in you with gladness. With his love, he will calm all your fears. He will rejoice over you with joyful songs."

Fear For My Children:

Do you fear your kids being involved in unforeseen accidents or associating with the wrong group of friends? One memory remains vivid: years ago, we took our young daughters on a journey to Ireland to see family. High above the crashing waves in the north, the Carrick-a-rede rope bridge is a popular tourist attraction that makes you feel the wind whipping past your face. This bridge bounces and sways precariously 100 feet above the crashing waves and jagged rocks. With each step closer to the bridge, the wind whistling through its gaps growing louder, my heart cried out, *NO! I can't risk my daughters crossing this rickety old bridge; it looks like it might collapse at any moment. A misstep could send them plummeting to their deaths.* My heart hammered against my ribs, a frantic drumbeat accompanying the dawning understanding of something I'd never comprehended before. Their destinies were not mine to command; only God possessed such power.

Witnessing my children's growth and development through both joyful and challenging times has solidified my belief that they are a gift from God. We raise them, guiding their development, and impart wisdom through countless teachings and shared moments. These gifts belong to us only because God has placed them in our care; a sacred trust. Instead of striving to control every aspect of their lives, our role is to surrender them to God's guidance and trust in His plan. Lift them up in prayer, teach them about the Lord with compassion, and trust God's will, however challenging.

Bible Promises:

Isaiah 44:3-4 (NIV); "3 For I will pour water on the thirsty land, and streams on the dry ground; I will pour out my Spirit on your offspring, and my blessing on your descendants. 4 They will spring up like grass in a meadow, like poplar trees by flowing streams."

Prayer:

Father, I am grateful for the privilege of raising my children and sharing life's journey with them. Thank You for guiding me during those precious years I spent with my children. Today, I will release them into Your care and guidance. I know

You will fight for them and delight in them, as You do for each of us. May blessings of health, happiness, and safety be upon them always. Let Your joyful presence fill them with light. May Your will be done, and may I find the strength to embrace whatever lies ahead.

Action Items:

What situations in your children's lives cause you the most fear?

_____

_____

_____

_____

How can you learn to surrender your children into God's care?

_____

_____

_____

_____

Meditate and memorize today's verse. How can this verse strengthen your faith in times of fear?

_____

_____

_____

_____

When you finish this devotional, come back and record your successes.

_____

_____

_____

_____

Psalm for fear and anxiety:

Psalm 127:3 (NLT); "Children are a gift from the Lord; they are a reward from him."

Day Eighteen: Fear of Greed

Verse for meditation:
Luke 12:15 (NIV); "Then he said to them, 'Watch out! Be on your guard against all kinds of greed; life does not consist in an abundance of possessions.'"

Fear of Greed:
A Christian's fear of greed comes from the Bible's harsh warnings against it, portraying it as a selfish lust for wealth that eclipses faith, damaging relationships with God and others, and often described as a destructive "love of money" that corrodes the soul.

The recognition of one's capacity for greed can be a powerful catalyst for self-reflection, motivating the practice of generosity and contentment to temper this inner struggle. Christians, as responsible stewards of God's abundant resources, are called to manage their wealth wisely, ensuring it doesn't dominate their lives or values.

Contentment acts as an antidote, neutralizing the poison of greed within the heart. Practice thanking God for all aspects of your life, recognizing His hand in both the joyful moments and the challenges. 1 Timothy 6:17-19 says to instruct those who are rich in the present age not to be arrogant or to set their hope on the uncertainty of wealth, but on God, who richly provides us with all things to enjoy. We see in Matthew 10:29, "Are not two sparrows sold for a penny? And yet not one of them will fall to the ground apart from your father. But the very hairs of your head are all numbered. So do not fear; you are more valuable than many sparrows." God cherishes us and will always supply our needs, offering comfort and sustenance.

Bible Promises:
Proverbs 11:28 (NIV); "Those who trust in their riches will fall, but the righteous will thrive like a green leaf."

Prayer:
Beloved Father above, we humbly come before You in prayer. Today, I humbly seek Your aid in purging the deceptive stems of greed that twist within my soul. Let my heart yearn only for You, a hunger that surpasses any worldly desire. Show me that material possessions and authority are not enough to satisfy my soul. You are my sustenance, my everything, providing all that I require. In Jesus' name. Amen.

Action Items:
Write about an item that you crave more than you think you should:

_____
_____
_____
_____
_____

How can you increase generosity in your life?

_____
_____
_____
_____

Meditate on and memorize today's verse. How can this verse strengthen your faith in times of fear?

_____
_____
_____
_____

When you finish this devotional, come back and record your successes.

_____
_____
_____
_____

Psalm for fear and anxiety:
Palm 37:16 (NIV); "Better the little that the righteous have than the wealth of many wicked."

Day Nineteen: Fear of Getting Old

Verse for meditation:
Proverbs 16:31 (NIV); "Gray hair is a crown of splendor; it is attained in the way of righteousness."

Fear of Getting Old:
Now that I'm in my sixties, waking up means battling the stiffness in my joints and the persistent throb in my lower back. The constant barrage of medical ads targeting my age group, each one highlighting the increased risks of aging with urgent, somber tones, only serves to increase my anxiety. My husband and I often joke, with a mix of laughter and a touch of weariness, that growing old is not for the faint of heart; the aches and pains are a daily reminder.

For Christians, the fear of aging can stem from worries about waning physical strength, and the dread of losing our purpose and feeling less useful in God's service, as well as the thought of a diminished ability to serve. The good news is that God does not have a "use before" date for His service.

Noah lived to be a remarkable 950 years old, and God used him to rebuild the earth after the devastating flood, a task that spanned generations. Abraham lived to be 175 years old, a long and blessed life, and God made him the father of the Israelite nation. Growing old is a true privilege, a testament to time well-spent, a blessing not everyone receives. And we can continue to serve the Lord, our hearts full of faith, regardless of age or the aches and pains in our aging bodies. The enduring promises of Isaiah 46:4, "Even to your old age and gray hairs I am he, I am he who will sustain you. I have made you and I will carry you; I will sustain you and I will rescue you," give me comfort, and I pray they do for you as well.

Bible Promises:
Isaiah 46:4 (NIV); "Even to your old age and gray hairs I am he, I am he who will sustain you. I have made you and I will carry you; I will sustain you and I will rescue you."

Prayer:
Dear God, as the years relentlessly march on, grant me the strength to greet the inevitable changes of aging with quiet acceptance, not fear. Guide me to cherish the wisdom and lessons learned throughout life, and to discover happiness in everyday moments, appreciating the simple things. May I continue to serve you and others with a grateful heart, even as my aging body slows and my strength fades, offering

what I can with every breath. Amen.

Action Items:

Write about ways you can continue to serve God as you age:

_____

_____

_____

_____

How can you stay flexible and prepared for the future?

_____

_____

_____

_____

Meditate and memorize today's verse. How can this verse strengthen your faith in times of fear?

_____

_____

_____

_____

When you finish this devotional, come back and record your successes.

_____

_____

_____

_____

Psalm for fear and anxiety:

Psalm 92:12-15 (NIV); "12 The righteous will flourish like a palm tree, they will grow like a cedar of Lebanon; 13 planted in the house of the Lord, they will flourish in the courts of our God. 14 They will still bear fruit in old age, they will stay fresh and green, 15 proclaiming, 'The Lord is upright; he is my Rock, and there is no wickedness in him.'"

Day Twenty: Fear of Being a Burden

Verse for meditation:
Galatians 6:2 (NIV); "Carry each other's burdens, and in this way you will fulfill the law of Christ."

Fear of Being a Burden:
The constant stream of information on X (formerly Twitter) keeps me engaged, a blur of tweets and notifications. Often, with a hesitant tone and apologetic expression, people will ask for prayer, prefacing their request with phrases like, "I'm sorry to ask, but I need prayer," or "Sorry to be a burden, but can you pray for me?" Such statements strike at the core of this fear: becoming a burden to others, a fear that manifests as a knot in the stomach. From our earliest years, we're instilled with a strong sense of self-reliance, taught to value independence and avoid being a burden on others.

In Christianity, the fear of burdening others contradicts the core teaching of "bearing one another's burdens," a teaching that emphasizes mutual support and understanding during hardship, urging Christians to take part in carrying each other's emotional and physical weight. When we keep our struggles hidden, we miss out on the deep bond that vulnerability creates among fellow Christians. We block the fulfillment of God's plan for others, leaving them deprived of the blessings He intended for them.

Sharing burdens within a loving, covenant community transforms the weight into something bearable, even uplifting. Mutual support and carrying one another's burdens are integral to the Christian community's identity and purpose, reflecting their shared faith and commitment to service. To be a member of Christ's body means sharing the burdens, the sorrows and struggles of others. When we bear one another's burdens, we experience the tangible weight of shared suffering, mirroring Christ's love and its immeasurable grace. As we share each other's burdens, we encounter the living Christ, feeling His presence and becoming more like Him. Allow others to ease your burden; don't be afraid to accept their help.

Bible Promises:
James 5:16 (NIV): "Therefore confess your sins to each other and pray for each other so that you may be healed. The prayer of a righteous person is powerful and effective."

Prayer:
Dear God, when the crushing weight of my burdens threatens to suffocate me, and the fear of being a burden to others consumes me, please remind me You are my

unwavering strength and my safe refuge. I release my worries into Your loving hands, trusting in Your strength to bear the weight of them all. Grant me the courage to lean on You, finding solace in the unwavering peace of Your endless love and tender care. Amen.

Action Items:

Write about a burden that you can share with someone else:

_____
_____
_____
_____

How can you share the burdens of others?

_____
_____
_____
_____

Meditate and memorize today's verse. How can this verse strengthen your faith in times of fear?

_____
_____
_____
_____

When you finish this devotional, come back and record your successes.

_____
_____
_____
_____

Psalm for fear and anxiety:

Psalm 68:19 (NIV); "Praise be to the Lord, to God our Savior, who daily bears our burdens."

Day Twenty-One: Fear of Being Scammed

Verse for meditation:
Luke 6:30 (NIV); "Give to everyone who asks you, and if anyone takes what belongs to you, do not demand it back."

Fear of Being Scammed:
A high-pitched chirp from your phone announced a message. A distant friend, citing unforeseen circumstances, requested money. Moved by Christian compassion, you contributed funds, requesting repayment at their convenience. Silence followed, your calls unanswered, texts unreturned, and the friend vanished from your life. The situation left you feeling scammed, betrayed, and deeply wary of future requests for money. But what principles of giving, from generosity to stewardship, does the Bible lay out for us to follow?

Our meditation verse instructs us to give generously to all who request aid. But many of us fear being scammed. The chilling thought of losing our hard-earned money is a constant worry. For a Christian, this fear arises from the conflict between the Bible's emphasis on trust and the harsh reality of malicious people who might exploit that trust, causing a constant tug-of-war between faith and caution. The Bible speaks of extending trust and generosity, but it also speaks caution, emphasizing the importance of careful consideration and sound judgment.

Being Christlike and turning the other cheek doesn't mean being naïve, like a doormat, allowing others to exploit our compassion and kindness. Jesus, in His human form, felt every emotion we experience and more, ultimately conquering them all. Through His examples, God shows how to repurpose negative situations to create tangible benefits for others. By understanding forgiveness, scams can unexpectedly turn into blessings in disguise. The challenges and triumphs you face don't dictate your identity; instead, they contribute to your growth and development. Remember the unwavering, boundless love God has for you defines you. God's grace has absolved your past sins, offering a path to emulate His boundless mercy.

Bible Promises:
Romans 12:19 (NIV); "Do not take revenge, my dear friends, but leave room for God's wrath, for it is written: 'It is mine to avenge; I will repay,' says the Lord."

Prayer:
Precious Lord and Creator. When con artists try to trick us, we turn to You for help, feeling the weight of their schemes pressing down. Soften our hearts to

understand the unspoken needs of others, and to discern their true intentions, even when hidden beneath a surface of words or actions. You forgive our transgressions, Lord, so guide us to extend that same grace to those who offend us. In Jesus' name. Amen.

Action Items:

Write about a time when you felt someone scammed you:

_____
_____
_____
_____

How can you forgive someone who has cheated you?

_____
_____
_____
_____

Meditate and memorize today's verse. How can this verse strengthen your faith in times of fear?

_____
_____
_____
_____

When you finish this devotional, come back and record your successes.

_____
_____
_____
_____

Psalm for fear and anxiety:

Psalm 37:5-6 (NIV); "5 Commit your way to the Lord; trust in him and he will do this: 6 He will make your righteous reward shine like the dawn, your vindication like the noonday sun."

Wrapping Up

Now that our twenty-one days of battling our fears have ended, let me summarize some key verses to help you live a life where you want to bring all your fears to God.

- God is with us and will never forsake us. Isaiah 41:10 (NIV); "So do not fear, for I am with you; do not be dismayed, for I am your God. I will strengthen you and help you; I will uphold you with my righteous right hand."
- God will guide us when we turn our fears over to Him. Proverbs 3:5-7 (NIV); "5 Trust in the Lord with all your heart and lean not on your own understanding; 6 in all your ways submit to him, and he will make your paths straight. 7 Do not be wise in your own eyes; fear the Lord and shun evil."
- God is the only one who can really change our circumstances; Psalm 56:3-4 (NIV); "3 When I am afraid, I put my trust in you. 4 In God, whose word I praise—in God I trust and am not afraid. What can mere mortals do to me?"
- God stands ready to help us conquer our fears when we seek Him. Psalm 34:4 (NIV); "I sought the Lord, and he answered me; he delivered me from all my fears."

We can also look at all the names of God throughout the Bible so we can know more of who God is and find the comfort we need to trust Him with our fears. Jehovah is:

- Elohim–our strong creator.
- Elyon–Lord, most high.
- Adonai–my master.
- Nissi–a banner over me.
- Rapha–my healer.
- Elolam–the everlasting God.
- Elroi–the God who sees me.
- Sabboth–Lord of host.
- Rohi–my shepherd.
- Tsideknu–our righteousness.
- Shalom–our peace.
- Chereb–our sword.
- Elkanna–a jealous God.
- Ezer–my help.
- Avinu–our father.

- Hashopet–our judge.
- Ori–my light.
- Elgibbor–the mighty God.
- Immeka–the Lord is with us.
- Elnose–the God that forgives.
- Jireh–our provider.

Everyone experiences fear from time to time. It's a natural human emotion. Fear is a common emotion that we all experience in various forms. To overcome your fears, you need to understand where they stem from and turn them over to God to find support to navigate them. Our God is aware of your situation and will supply you with whatever is needed for your journey forward. I pray these words, Bible verses, and God's names serve as a balm to your soul, easing the anxieties and fears that this world throws at you.

So, if fear is one extreme, what is the opposite of fear? Peace, most specifically, the peace of God. Our fears may remain, but with God's unwavering support, we can transcend our anxieties and experience the serenity of His peace. John 16:33 in the NIV translation reads: "I have told you these things, so that in me you may have peace. In this world, you will have trouble. But take heart! I have overcome the world." Our Heavenly Father is the Prince of Peace (Isaiah 9:6) and He will not withhold His peace from those who believe in Him. The end is not fear; rather, it's an invitation to find strength and peace in God, a sanctuary from the chaos where faith replaces dread.

Philippians 4:6-7 (NIV); "6 Do not be anxious about anything, but in every situation, by prayer and petition, with thanksgiving, present your requests to God. 7 And the peace of God, which transcends all understanding, will guard your hearts and your minds in Christ Jesus."

Shalom.

ABOUT THE AUTHOR

Yvonne M. Morgan is an award-winning Christian author, blogger, and storyteller with a passion for inspiring faith and compassion through her writing. She is the author of heartfelt children's books, including *Mary the Missionary: A Kenyan Adventure*, as well as Christian devotionals and inspirational works for adults. Drawing from her experiences in global mission work, Yvonne weaves stories that encourage readers—both young and old—to live with purpose, kindness, and a heart for serving others. When she's not writing, Yvonne advocates for orphans and vulnerable children through Orphan Relief Effort, sharing God's love across cultures and generations.

THANK YOU!

Thank you for reading this book from Mt. Zion Ridge Press.

If you enjoyed the experience, learned something, gained a new perspective, or made new friends through story, could you do us a favor and write a review on Goodreads or wherever you bought the book?

Thanks! We and our authors appreciate it.

We invite you to visit our website, MtZionRidgePress.com, and explore other titles in fiction and non-fiction. We always have something coming up that's new and off the beaten path.

And please check out our podcast, **Books on the Ridge,** where we chat with our authors and give them a chance to share what was in their hearts while they wrote their book, as well as fun anecdotes and glimpses into their lives and experiences and the writing process. And we always discuss a very important topic: *Tea!*

You can listen to the podcast on our website or find it at most of the usual places where podcasts are available online. Please subscribe so you don't miss a single episode!

Thanks for reading. We hope you come back soon!